THOMAS AR

PEACEFUL SOLUTIONS

LIVING-CIRCLE .mittelstand.de

About this book:

"This book is the introduction, into the sum of the deep handed down 'secrets' of all original cultures. It is the entry point for the path to a greater understanding of truth. It does not teach, but lets you experience what many people are really looking for. It is the beginning of your journey, in the footsteps of Parsival, Hercules, Jesus, Buddha, Mohammed and many others. Here, with a 'simple' series of books, begins the until-now hidden path which can create a real world in which you and the next seven generations can build their felt reality."
Guido Eickhoff

About the Author:

Thomas Arcuelo
Séh shé yeñ Goh or "White Eagle"

He represents the territory of Upstate New York USA and walks in the tradition of the Iroquois Nations . He carries the wisdom of the "Great Law of Peace and the Law of Seeding". He specialises in communication, indigenous natural sciences, indigenous medicine and mental health.

Thomas Arculeo was raised in two worlds from the age of 6: In the care of the elders and several medical circles of the Haudenosaunee (Iroquois), Five Nations and that of the Roman Catholic Church, who initiated him on the one hand into the Indigenous Natural Sciences and on the other hand into the secrets of Catholicism.

At the same time, at the age of seven, he met his 72-year-old Shaolin master, who trained him in medical chi gong, among other things. He practised this until he was 30 years old in New York State. On his further path of ancient knowledge, he met his Kriya Yoga master from Badrinath, India and thus followed the path of many great masters and elders of many eras and cultures.

Initiated and trained in the natural science disciplines of four different cultures, his childhood was not associated with play, but marked by daily hard training and discipline, always with the intention of grasping medical knowledge.

During his 12 years of study at different faculties and universities in the fields of human medicine and psychology, he worked in-parallel for his family business, making aircraft instruments for the commercial and military aircraft industry.

This legacy of the wilderness and nature are still his sources of strength and his everlasting drive. It is his goal to make the culmination of his knowledge attainable for everyone via simple methods and to teach them how to implement it in their daily lives

Peaceful Solutions

[Thomas Arculeo]

First limited edition 12/12/2022 - Copyright Thomas Arculeo
Second limited edition 12/12/2023 - Copyright Thomas Arculeo
Third edition 08/2024 - Copyright Thomas Arculeo

Publisher: LIVING-CIRCLE.mittelstand.de
Translation: Guido Eickhof
Cover image: Thomas Arculeo
Illustrations: Guido Eickhoff
Publisher: "BoD · Books on Demand GmbH, In de Tarpen 42,
22848 Norderstedt".
Printed by: "Libri Plureos GmbH, Friedensallee 273, 22763 Hamburg"

ISBN: 978-3-7597-5912-2

Bibliographic information of the German National Library: The German National Library lists this publication in the German National Bibliography; detailed bibliographic data is available on the Internet at dnb.dnb.de.

VOLUME 1

LIVING-CIRCLE .mittelstand.de

Acknowledgement

Many thanks to.

Michaela, Rafaela, Ursula, Oliver, Andreas and all those who accompanied and supported the physical development process of this book. And especially to my mother, Lorriane, who Adopted me when I was 10 days old and supported me. To all of the Iroquois Elders and Clan Mothers who have Taught me and guided me, my chief, Leon Shenandoah, clanmother Audrey Shenandoah and many more. Thank you Barbara Argyle.

By way of introduction

As an entrepreneur, consultant and trainer for the European Union, ministries, institutes and small and medium-sized enterprises, I have experienced several paradigm shifts and partly helped to shape them. In the last two decades, the increasing challenges of people and companies have determined my personal research drive for innovative solutions for both humans and their family´s, and their businesses.

From personality, language, culture and consciousness research, to neuroscience, psychology, alternative healing methods and many more, I still found a lack after many trainings, experiences and applications. That is, until I encountered the legacy of knowledge and the deep teachings of the ancient masters in ancient cultures. But true source knowledge is rare. But then I met Thomas Arculeo.

When I met Thomas, only then did the path begin to realising the deeper meaning of the Old High German language. Old High German was the metaphorical language of the Druids and the teaching path of the Germanic knowledge bearers. The figurative language was the true knowledge transporter of spiritual masters and the guardian of the knowledge of indigenous Europe and their natural science, as well as in cultures worldwide. In this, I have recognized the problem with the modern German language.

In the figurative language, the metaphorical underlies the deeper meaning of the oral traditions. This is where the transfer of true knowledge takes place. Thomas always emphasised, "Before you begin to translate these texts, you must experience the meaningfulness in your own body."

But getting started was not easy, despite much prior training. Through his years of practice in the cultural association of a wide variety of teaching disciplines, such as the North American medical associations, the Kriya Yoga of the Himalayan teachers, and the medical Qi-Gong of Buddhist Shaolin monks, which Thomas has been practising intensively for 50 years, he was able to find the way to convey this knowledge in an understandable modern language.

An encounter with a guardian of knowledge has an intensity and a lightness, but also demands patience. Accompanying Thomas in the implementation of his sentences, my own process of realisations began. The power of words is crucial here. Every sentence, every paragraph is a lesson. I became even more aware of this through the "translation" of this book.

Through this process, I noticed the complications with the modern language and I tried to solve them partly typographically or with illustrations. Through the intensive exercises even I, as a "translator", have difficulties to translate the oral traditions into modern Language and to make them understandable for those of European heritage.

This book is more of a journey and a practical manual for every reader. It is a path we walk together.

This book is an introduction and also a taste of how to simplify your daily life and thought structures with an expanded consciousness. Sometimes I still had to formulate a sentence for myself or pause to let it take effect. Then it slowly came into the mind. Sometimes very suddenly, sometimes much later. This kind of communication was used in everyday life throughout indigenous Europe and is its true natural science. Since then, I have become more and more aware of the lightness within that many seem to lack.

We hope that each reader enjoys his own evolution and thus becomes part of a conscious and relaxed social paradigm shift. That collectively, we become a society that develops more humane and modern economic and social systems. Through this encounter and these practices, I recognize the key that is sought by many people in Europe and especially in the German middle class. Step by step we want to accompany you and our community into a positive future.

"What it means to touch a paper and the soul of a tree, made you aware how connected we are. Not only with our environment, but with the intelligence of the universe."

Guido Eickhoff/"Translator"

More books in this series:

Volume- 1 - Intro

Subsequent volumes:

Volume - 2 - I

Volume - 3 - We

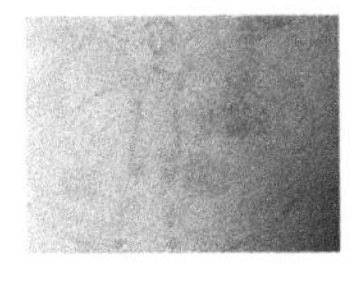

Volume - 4 - The 5 elements

Volume -5 - (0)

Operating instructions

This book is the self-experiencing introduction to the legacy of the Druids and Elders of the world.

The entire series of books is an instructional path of the ancient way of the Masters, as it was passed down orally in the past.

This book is a written translation of the oral ways of the Old Masters and their school.

The author translates, in writing, the experiences his teachers have explained to him through the oral tradition and practical application.

Only through intensive exercises and practices was it possible for him to translate these teachings into written form, whereby the path to self-knowledge has become the key to understanding.

During the translations we came across stumbling blocks that are difficult to express in modern European tongues, because the legacy of the Old High Languages such as English, German, Celtic and Flemmish have been increasingly lost.

Where metaphoric language - as multidimensional allegory is used to guide the student into his own processes, cuts had to be made, which will be explained in more detail in the following volumes.

Footnote: This book is the introduction of the book volumes 1 to 5, in the second volume with the title "I" one gains a deeper insight into the meaning of the different "I".Here the author uses the Old High German term "I" as Trinity.

You - the tree - and "I"

TABLE OF CONTENTS

THE SEED

"Every thought is a Seed,

every word the Soil

in which the Thought

begins to grow."

Welcome!

We can tell a story

as a "dream" or as a "reality"

in every moment and

in every "breath",

when the consciousness of the soul

expands.

[For your notes]

When you read this text (symbols), please consider the word "I" as its original meaning, from the "Old High German trinity form (which was introduced into the english language in the year 1150[1])". Thereby "I" is always meant as a trinity - your body, your spirit and your soul as a unified being. This means seeing and feeling an inseparable trinity, three/3 beings in one "I". As part of the planet, the universe and the spirit of creation.

If you, yes you, a "human being", inseparable from your body, your mind and your soul, try to translate this text or better these symbols as an interpreter, so that they are filled into a form that fits into your reality, you as a "trinity" will notice changes in how you look at and feel the world in the future...

You are the interpreter and translator of the following symbols. Don't forget, letters are symbols with a deeper meaning. Your life experience determines their meaning and how your soul and emotions translate these symbols. All your senses are also stimulated and addressed. You are the one who is addressed, as an interpreter and not as a "reader".

This space was created for you to write personal notes. To write down your thoughts, feelings and perceptions and to record your "translations". Enjoy the journey in this introduction to the books in volumes 1 to 5.

---

[1] Oxford English Dictionary: https://www.oed.com/dictionary/i_pron?tab=factsheet#1073073

Emotions rise, vibrations and relationships develop. Is this my physical reality? Or is it just a dream?

When "I" write this book, using the term "we", you, the reader, have guided my hand to bring the symbols to the soul of the tree, the paper from which these pages are made.

When "we" touch these pages, "we" are connected to the soul and pure essence of the "tree" and all plant life.

This paper lives when it touches our fingers.

It transmits all our emotions when "we" place the symbols that you call letters and lay them on the skin of the tree.

Touch these pages gently. Smell them, absorb the essence of the natural cycles and realise that it is not possible to be separated from the beauty of the absolute truth.

The simplest of all human processes is the process of simply being alive and vibrant in each moment. To be consciously connected, to experience the full potential of each moment, and to understand the concept of nature in every cell of the body.

[For your notes]

The smell of maple, oak, willow, sassafras, birch, walnut, cherry and pine, the sound of otters playing in a pond, and feeling the softness of people's hands when they touch our skin, like this thin piece of paper.

To see life through the eyes of the great pine tree is to see life as perfect harmony (non-dual, no judgement) that supports all beings and treats them as ONE. (You - the tree - and I) will write this book together in peace.

THE SEED

"Breathe in. ... Slowly ...

Isn't it true that now a thought is forming as a seed?"

Being Born.

„The Seed"

"Breathe out. ... Slowly ...

Is it fertile soil in which this seed grows?

A mixture of emotions, desires, things that you will manifest.

What is it that wants to grow within you?

Will the seed end up in the flour mill or will it become a thriving meadow for generations to come?

[For your notes]

We all live in coexistence on a spinning blue ball, a true playground for the five basic elements that created everything physical and non-physical.

Everything physical is in reality more or less nothing - but when "we" see, smell, touch, taste and feel, the physical becomes your reality, existing only for a very short moment in the present form.

Even I, "the great tree" who sacrificed my body to create this paper, who is thousands of years old, have experienced many changes, the physical exists only for a short moment, a moment without beginning and without end.

While *we* create the symbols on this thin piece of paper, *you* are the translator who gives life to the symbols and the paper.

You, yes you, the reader, become the translator/gardener.

"All people have gathered the material for their physical body from the same place and material that created the bodies of all physical things, even my body is formed from the same source that creates your body. "

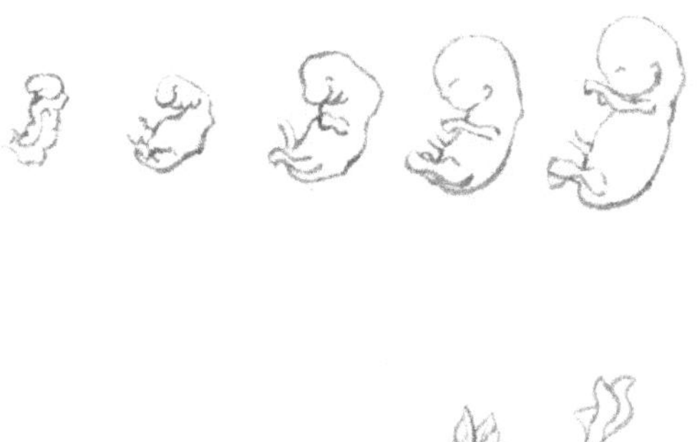

I give my fallen leaves to the smallest creatures so that the whole family of nature can exist. You also benefit from this process.

"Is it your intelligence that transforms a piece of bread into a human form?"

It was not possible for you to touch this ever-loving intelligence, letting your connection with all living things flow together, was it?

Why do we use the physical bodies of trees and plants to create this very thin piece of skin we call paper? The Ancient cultures used oral transfer of Wisdom and knowledge, they had great respect for all living things.

Is cutting down entire forests, where thousands upon thousands of living beings have to die for your comfort and peaceful life, the truth? Or have you just forgotten that you are in constant connection with the "soul" of existence and the forest?

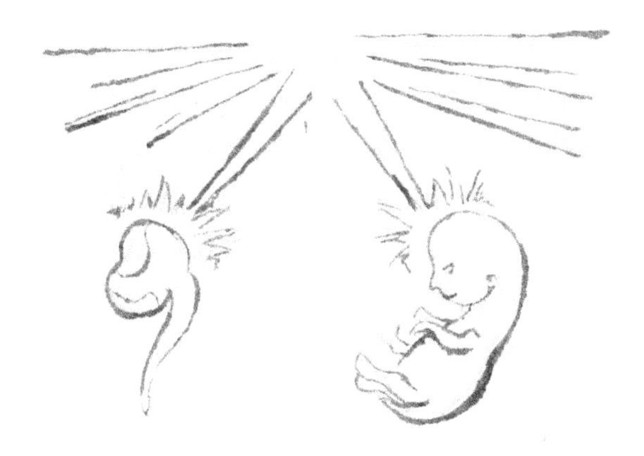

Your consciousness has always had access to the source of emotional interpretation since the beginning of time. When our physical bodies were smaller than a grain of sand, something happened to every single particle of existence, even thoughts.

A very small piece of "male fire," that you can call *light,* gave you the signal to create. You, the human being, began your existence in an ocean, in the womb of your mother.

Within the first three months you experienced every aspect of evolution, expanding rapidly until you reached the Human form.

[For your notes]

We gathered particles to create and build a house for our souls. The tree, the roses, the worms, the fish, the chickens, the grass you eat (bread), the cows, even your own car began with the same process, as a stone taken from the body of this spinning blue ball.

"The soul of the great peace tree"

Original drawing: Thomas

The breath.

Pause. Breathe in and while doing so count. 1 - 2 - 3 - 4 - - to 24

Your physical being is made up of the same materials that are under your feet. It is the portion of the elements and vibrations that make up "matter" - everything that is physical.

If you could not use your eyes for a moment, if you were blind, could you still communicate through the soul of the great tree?

This adventure is yours if you choose to continue reading.

Do you want to touch the soul of the skin of the great tree? Close your eyes and read with your soul, with your heart, with the truth, without words.

Be grateful that you have the opportunity to experience oneness in every cell of your body.

[For your notes]

Thank you for opening your eyes!

Your breath has changed, what do you feel now? What do you hear? I hear my breath leaving my body. You are breathing inward through your lungs. We are "one", "synchronised" in every breath. When you breathe outward, I thank you for the nutrients I need to build my body.

Come with your eyes closed and smell this paper and touch my soul. The "soul of the great peace tree", which is addressed to all who are in search of truth.

Come and smell the soul - because that is all that is left of me. It is the portion of water that transports me. Paper has between 14% and 17% water, enough to transport my soul. Sweetness, gentleness.

I am waiting to experience the oneness with your soul.

"Light is full of passengers"

But what is it that we experience together?

Is it the experience of life, of being alive, of being able to experience "thoughts" and memories?

You are "human", that is, you are created by your emotions, the vibration of the ocean under your skin.

In the morning mirror, "You" see that it is the only way to experience "Me" (soul of the tree) as a kind of defined concept of interpretation, while the smell of coffee fills the kitchen.

We as "THREE" (You, I and the soul of the tree) as one "I AM" reflect from the mirror.

[For your notes]

What does the "I AM" in the mirror say when "YOU" try to see "I AM" as "My Self"?

What if what we see is only light?

Light that is reflected and not absorbed and we are not able to use the free energy of the reflecting light. Our relationship is then lost with this.

If we want to create a unity to form emotional gratitude and harmony in our outer world, it is up to you to interpret the passengers of light, emotionally, mentally and physically. This is where your reflection comes into being.

Your interpretation of the passengers, forms a unity in the mirror world of the outer world.

The mirror world is only your interpretation of the outer world, the world of us THREE.

[For your notes]

Light is full of passengers, vibration causes movement = Breath makes "I" able to be experienced, but "I" as the "I" pushing the pen and forming symbols that creates movement and definition and you as the "I" and emotional translator of these symbols.

We or "I" can express the events of thought while observing the happening of the light in the bathroom mirror while breathing synchronised, in harmony together, "I" and "ME" together as "I AM" = One.

Or we go to the kitchen and make ourselves a ham and egg toastie with fried potatoes, but today I opt for a smoothie, two bananas fried in coconut oil with ground black pepper and a touch of maple syrup. But we always face each other.

[For your notes]

The mirror can only reflect. If you close your eyes, there is no reflection to be seen. Does that mean that "I" ceases to exist?

"I" exists only because "we" exist. "We" are "I AM", "I" can translate "I AM" only as a reflection of "Us", "We" the true physical self as an organism created from and through a subtle balance and play of the five elements of nature. The balance of these elements is the balance of all creation, in all universes.

When we experience the "ME" as brushing its teeth, while the toaster browns the toast and fills the room with a bouquet of emotions, while the aroma of toast and coffee fills the air and the birds sing to the sunrise.

The "I" experiences the fundamental vibration of being alive in the form of the "I" defined by millions of years of evolution

[For your notes]

"I" to become "ME", breathing together in the mirror.

Please do not forget that "I" am holding this pen and pressing the ink into the symbols. "I" have just begun to breathe inward, slowly, aware of the whole breath, - through both sides of the nose, peacefully, breathing inward, filling "my" lungs, expanding into every corner, counting slowly

one------two------ three ------- four ------- five ----- six -----to 24.

letting go a little and resting, holding your breath and counting again

one------two------ three ------- four ------- five ----- six -----to 24.

Then exhale through both sides of the nose – releasing the waste that accumulated during the breath hold. "I" must experience "I AM", without "I AM", "I" exists without manifestation.

Breathing, thinking, creating

[For your notes]

"I" as the person who presses the ink also defines the emotional translations that "You", the "One" who interprets the journey through all the accumulated memories of information that the emotional translation of these symbols has developed.

This is the point where "I" as "One", the "Human" or "Identity" puts these symbols on the skin of a tree.

But you, the translator, should stop now, take a walk outside, breathe the air, live as you are, experience that you are "One" without judgement. See the smiles on the faces of children; see the happiness of a newly married couple. Loving, caring, longing for a peaceful future. A squirrel runs up a maple tree, the sweet scent of autumn leaves fills every breath, while the morning mist lifts up from the deep valleys.

"This is how each "I" created the "WE"."

"I", the sunlight with many passengers, can flow into every cell of your body when you breathe inward - inhale "I" as your form. It is your physical form that expresses "I". Vibrate with "I" as the form of "You." It is your physical form that expresses "I". Vibrate with "I" with pure life.

When the crows begin their morning gathering, the sunlight breaks through the fog, - your coffee and tea is ready, life around you is full of vibrant colours and smells, the sweetness of autumn leaves captured on the water of the fog.

Inhale, act, exhale.

The "I" and the vibration "I AM" create "Us" or "We". Thus, each "I" has created the "WE".

The great tree is also "I", it has "I AM" "as a tree".

The same is true for the search for a single identity, the search for the "I".

"Does the candle see the flame?"

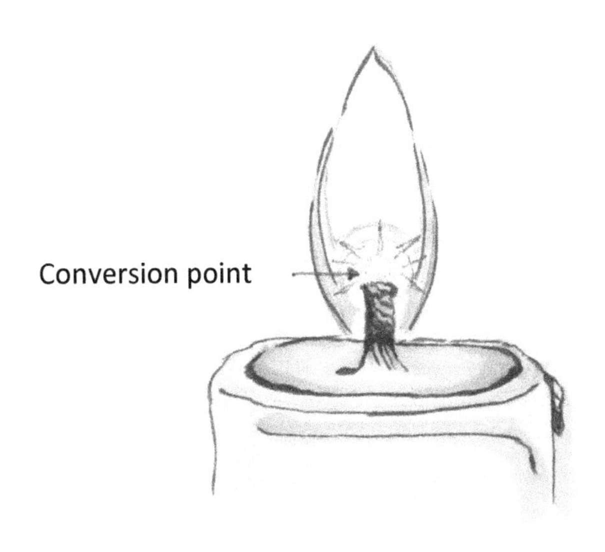

The candle is the food of the Flame. Light is the chain reaction or the product of chain reactions.

If you still ask yourself the question who "I" am, the person who presses the ink into the symbols, we will say - I was born in a military hospital in Heidelberg. But "I" experienced birth much earlier, long before "I" decided to take the form of a little boy who greeted the outside world somewhere in Germany. "I" as light. The light of the heart of a little boy.

The little boy is irrelevant, he is only a translator.

In your mind you may want to make a picture of the little boy, but he was born blind. My light blinded him. He was pure. "I" as a small candle flame in the hearts of all living beings. "I" the light that makes it possible to experience the sweetness of being alive.

Footnote: This book is the introduction to volumes 1 to 5; in the second volume, entitled "I", we gain a deeper insight into the meaning of the various "I's." Here the author uses the Old High German term "I" as a trinity.

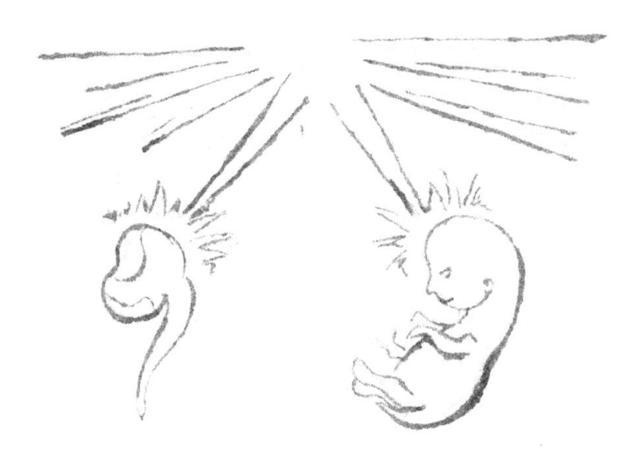

The same little spark that tells a seed to unfold sets off a chain reaction. As in every cell, every seed, every egg, every thought.

Do you feel how deep in your bones a new cell is born that starts to grow when a small spark of light gives it the signal to grow?

A simple gentle touch by a very small light.

Energy is the reaction that is triggered by this small spark of light. Energy is vibration. Vibration gathers particles and creates form. First vibration, then plasma, then liquid, then solid forms. Every cell in your body vibrates and works together to create a physical body that can translate the emotional vibration that binds you to these pages (the soul of the tree).

[For your notes]

Do you want to read (translate) some more? Or do you want to go shopping for dinner?

Zucchini stuffed with barley rice puree with cashew cream, endive salad with young potatoes and pumpkin seed oil, dinner for two? Then "We" will be in the kitchen for at least three hours, and here I leave you alone in your vibration.

Thank you for travelling with me.

You may now breathe outward.

One -- two --- three ---- four ----- five ------ six ------- to 24,

pause.

THE BREATH

"The breath as king, of the spirit, of the "we", of the "you" and of the "I".

Did you enjoy the food?

Try this simple exercise:

Breathe in through both sides of your nose, inhale gently and very slowly, close your eyes and think only of "WE".

"WE" as an acting experience, giving gratitude to all of creation by slowly filling your lungs to full capacity and stretching your spine skyward, staying deeply rooted in the core of this spinning blue ball.

Open your eyes only when inner peace and harmony have reached every cell of your body. Release the pressure in your lungs just enough to relax, and then hold your breath without holding it, simply relaxed.

[For your notes]

All thoughts are stopped, only what is under your skin, hidden from the optical perceptions of that which you call your physical body, that which is not influenced consciously by you.

Cells are born, digestive juices break down components to nourish your cells, and all of this is still happening unconsciously.

Close your eyes and feel what is best defined as the Lymphatic Ocean, the ocean in which we were fertilised as a very small, invisible cell, in the womb of a woman you now know as your mother, with a Ph between 7.4 and 8.9, relevant to our healthy existence.

What she thought, formed your mind.

What she felt, formed your character.

What she ate, formed your body.

[For your notes]

You, as the translator of these symbols, feel sensations under your skin as you hold your breath. You are trading oxygen, the (fire) that reaches from the smallest plankton in the oceans to the largest trees, forests and all plant life.

Your cells are being fed nutrients and energy, when your cells are done with this trade, then it is time to exchange your waste (Co2) that is so naturally "waiting" for "Us" and "You" to be released.

[For your notes]

Be aware of each breath,

Breathe in,

pause,

Breathe out,

pause,

trade.

Permanently trading, nourishing and in gratitude.

In the pause, the magic of the "we" takes place.

„The "nothing" exists only
in the form of the dual principles.“

You are the translator of these symbols, which are plant sap that flows down the needle and creates the contrast that makes it possible to see the symbols that you define as "letters" or signs. Or is "I" the one holding the needle and creating the black and white contrast that in some way affects not only your visual perception, but also your entire biological system.

Keep in mind that this form of communication would not be possible without the skin of the tree and the water in your lymphatic ocean, which allows the electromagnetic field to transmit the information you have translated into emotions that may have affected not only your own life, but will affect at least seven generations to come.

„You hold the soul of the forest in your hand.

Only together we will form plant sap into symbols, shape emotions that will become perceptible when you touch the skin of the tree."

-breath-

Here "I" will change the form of "We", "You", "I" and "The Tree" and use the symbols in a different context. In the form of "I", where "I" can be seen as the person holding the needle that forms the contrast of the symbols that you then translate.

"I" is an experience of you. Since "I" use the symbol "I", it is only you, the translator, who can give "I" an emotional definition.

[For your notes]

If "I" as the creator of the "ink" = plant sap, which enables us to communicate, if the "I" pushes the needle over the skin of the big tree, you will see that only a "we" is possible.

Existence is not only "I" and "you", or this and that. We are always connected with each other, and "WE" are constantly exchanging and influencing each other.

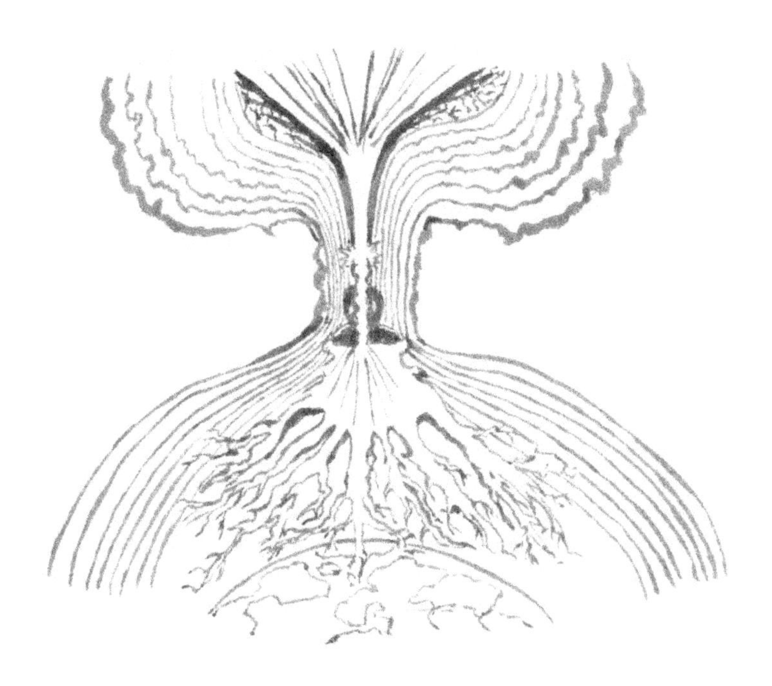

The "nothing" cannot exist.

The "nothing" exists only in the form of the dual principles.

To observe the nothingness, you need a physical body.... that makes it impossible to observe the "nothing", because the "nothing" disappears when you have consciousness, the nothing means No-Thing/No Thing... you can't experience that as a human being.

[For your notes]

Through your own physicality and the materials you are made of, with all your various ecosystems and electromagnetic fields, information and data processing centres, cameras, microphones, speakers, identification and analysis centres, distribution centres, hydraulic pressure regulators, electrical cable networks and stones, it is not possible to ignore the fact that you are a part of a very physical being, connected in many ways to the ecosystems that give you the form of a human being, even the space between you and the tree is full of passengers floating in a plasma that connects the whole creation.

Then who is the observer, who is the translator? How is it possible that "I" believe to be the only "I" standing in a great distance in front of the morning mirror in your bathroom?

"I" is in all existing matter.

Every particle of matter can only form because "I" can only be seen through "ME" as the manifested form that "YOU" defined when you opened your eyes before the morning mirror.

Did you know that this is the place where "WE" all meet?

When you open your eyes in front of the morning mirror, the light reflects your image. The light has passengers. These passengers are either "reflected or absorbed". It is the air in your breath that creates "I" as a physical form and the water in your eyes behind the lens that makes it possible for you to feel emotion and definition as "I" stand in front of the mirror, never forgetting that millions upon millions of tiny cells swim beneath your skin in your lymphatic ocean and help you create a sense of "I" as a "collective" that includes and is aware of the balances of life.

[For your notes]

Touch your skin with your eyes closed, breathe in and become aware of the complexity of the harmony of biological processes that make it possible to experience the "I".

Touch releases oxytocin, dopamine, theobromine, serotonin, and many emotional impulses that also release hormones that enable the "I" to experience the emotion of "me." "I" is just a sensation.

"You" as the translator of all these symbols experience the symbols as a complex digital code used for this conversation. Please do not forget that your Lymphatic Ocean has the ability to generate electromagnetic fields. The Ph levels of the Lymphatic Ocean determine how much electricity your body, heart and organs generate.

[For your notes]

-breathe-

You are able to experience what you think is life. Basically "I" or "you" only translate digital information. You in an electromagnetic field are with your bodies as only a collection of highly complex social systems which are connected by an electrical network which is very similar to the modern technical networks.

Your eyes are scanners or you can call them digital cameras, the ears are the microphones, the nose and tongue are receptors, the skin has over 72,000 receivers, all sense organs are permanently connected to what you define as the outside world, although there is no outside world in the actual physical sense.

What you define as your skin is nothing more than a filter that reacts to the finest electromagnetic differences and sends your body information generated by the outside world.

That which you call your consciousness is only electrical impulses which are transformed into a form of physical communication which enables you to react to the so-called outside world.

The experiment of touching this piece of paper, smelling this paper, connects "you" not only with "the soul of the tree", but also with my soul and the soul of the ink (plant sap) or some minerals from which some inks are made.

But also with all the people involved in the production process of the paper, the pen, the ink, and all those involved in the production of the factories, and the machines that make the paper, the pen, the ink, the printing machines, the paper cutting machines, and all the little parts of the machines, and your journey can go much further.

[For your notes]

Machines are made from stones that people have taken from the surface of the earth, also using machines made from the "hands of men".

A person's perception can be trained.

You, the translator of these symbols, think you have a concept of what you call "life" or "existence".

How many biological processes are going on in your body at this moment? Red blood cells are migrating from your lungs and transporting oxygen (fire) contained in the iron of these cells, one could also say rusty particles that work like small trucks and deliver their cargo

[For your notes]

After delivering their small packages, they collect waste products and bring them back to the lungs to be excreted through the nose and mouth.

But there is much more going on: the red blood cells have a core of cobalt and iron that stores small amounts of electricity (cosmic energy) or so-called solar energy, you could also call the red blood cells solar-charged energy cells or small batteries. The iron comes in contact with the oxygen and charges the battery.

But it goes further, vitamin B12 is in the nucleus of every cell that has a DNA coil in its nucleus, in the centre of this nucleus is a cobalt molecule that has the potential of a nuclear power plant if the Ph of your lymphatic ocean is between 7.8 and 9.4.

[For your notes]

-breathe-

The question arises:

"How can "I" reach this level"?

Only you can answer this question: How do you balance your consciousness? By choosing the food you eat and how consciously you breathe.

Green leaves with chlorophyll, fresh clean water and fresh fruits, grains and vegetables not overcooked, along with exercises that keep the lymphatic ocean moving.

There is a law in nature, the wisdom of the mountain - water that stands still is used to support new life. Water that has passed over 7 stones over 7 waterfalls is crystal clear and pure.

The clarity of the lymphatic ocean will clear after exercises such as yoga, swimming, tai chi, qi gong, stretching, dancing, movement and joy – proven.

Your magnetic charisma will increase.

Good health and mental condition is the result.

Your battery is recharged. Peace and harmony will fill your environment, remain flexible and strong.

THE LAW OF THE SEED

„The universal law of existence
- One plus one is always three -
The law of the seed“

Stagnant water is used.

The universal law of existence, as observed by the ancient Himalayan masters, is described in the following formula: "One plus one is always three," which is also considered the Genesis sequence. The ancient cultures call this, "The Law of the Seed."

Nothing in the universe exists without purpose. Most people do not know their purpose. Mother Earth is constantly creating. Everything on her skin and in her blood has a purpose that serves all forms. What you define as "death" does not exist. The physical form of your body is only borrowed for a short time, what you identify as your body is an accumulation of material borrowed from the surface of the "blue ball that spins". This is how the most complex ecosystem you can imagine is created.

[For your notes]

Your "Lymphatic Ocean" is full of organisms, all trying to work together in harmony to keep you alive.

When this balance is disturbed, your thought processes and behaviour change.

In the whole universe there is nothing called "duality", it is not possible that anything exists outside the processes of existence (cause and effect)!

Everything is a cycle .

"You" as a translator of these symbols may think in terms of good and bad. This type of consciousness and thought processes have created a relationship to something you define as "life and death".

You believe that your physical body keeps "you" alive, but this is not true. You exist as an entity, an energy form that uses the physical matter of Earth.

[For your notes]

- breathe -

If you want to continue to experience what you identify as emotions, you will use your so-called body to express something you call "life".

That which you define as "life" is trapped in the consciousness of duality, you believe in death only because your physical form will return to Earth, in a process you refer to as death.

„Consciousness is a form of energy"

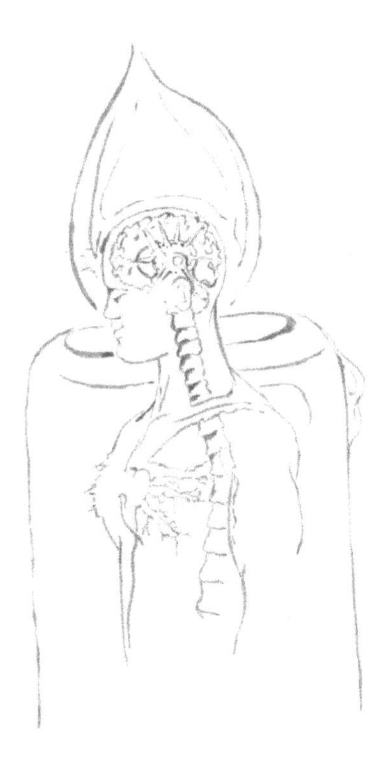

- breathe -

Consciousness is an energy form, immortal, without duality, constantly gathering information, constantly learning.

The fear of death is only the fear of the return of your physical body to the place where you borrowed it.

The microorganisms such as the cells that make up your musculature, circulatory system, and organs, as well as the millions upon millions of bacteria that keep the entire ecosystem intact, all have their own consciousness. They all have their own level of consciousness and are very happy that you are working with them to gather food and water.

[For your notes]

- breathe -

When you experience hunger, you are responding to the needs of all these little organisms. If you appreciate the existence of the many different groups of collective social structures, then you will realise the importance of "fair trade".

Choose the contents of the food consciously, because their effects on the behaviour patterns and communication between the cells, cause the different biotopes. What you call diseases is nothing else than a biotope that you have created through nutrition. You personally choose in which biotope you want to think and live. This effects that which you refer to as “Your Behaviour and thought Patterns” Do you think like swamp Parasites, or like a Human with clear thoughts and Loving behaviour?

"The skin is a highly interactive organ."

The skin.

It has a variable surface tension. Every thought, every emotion changes the surface tension. Every movement in the electromagnetic plasma changes the surface tension, sending information to your consciousness and creating an energy field that can become "hard as stone" through intense training practices still practised in all indigenous cultures.

There are tribes in Africa that have trained their bodies through dance, hard work, and mental makeup to be able to fend off high calibre bullets and direct sword thrusts without breaking their skin. These tribes were the most feared tribes. They protected many tribes of the West African Empire when the European colonists arrived. This is also trained in Shaolin temples and in southern India.

[For your notes]

At this point, "I" would like to speak to you about "imagination", "illusion" and "reality".

Drink a glass of water.

The surface tension changes, the thought patterns change, the reaction to the external world occurs, 72,000 Nadi,s or Nodes which can be seen as Handy-Masts are active and provide information to the water that is distributed throughout the lymphatic ocean.

As you read these previous words, a question or many questions may arise, such as "how can this be true, or why am I spending my precious time on this text?".

Such questions arise because the facts mentioned are far beyond your physical life experiences.

This is something far beyond what you have read (translated). These symbols were not even present in your experience and not in your imagination, but perhaps you have gathered images through watching movies that allow you to create associations. They leave you alone with your mind and your physical body, which means that your imagination and your limitations, leave you alone with your illusion.

[For your notes]

The illusion is rather a dream or a "morph" that can be brought into your own physical experience, or something that is capable of entering your reality if you accept it as true, or as a goal that can be achieved by anyone through proper mental and physical training. What else was part of everyday life in ancient indigenous cultures, you can experience for yourself without practising it in monasteries in China or India.

That which is physical is real. Take a stone in your hand, hold it closed, close your eyes, feel the warmth and then the pulse.

[For your notes]

That which is conceived and experienced through digital, multimedia presentations such as movies, news broadcasts, written texts, or conversations with friends remains in the vast caverns of your mind as imagination and illusion, leaving your mind with two choices:

Truth or non-truth.

Turning this into truth is not and I repeat, not truth unless you do the necessary training both mentally and physically. This information can be used in your personal life as a goal to achieve and then brought into the realm of your own personal experience.

Otherwise, this information will remain in your mind as a catalyst for your imagination and ego, which will remain in your mind as a very dangerous virus that has the ability to not only disrupt your physical and personal environment, but you will want to share these facts and information with your friends and family.

[For your notes]

Truth can be spread, information can be spread, illusion and fantasy is the food for your imagination. Information can be useful and brought into our physical experience.

But why is it that most of the information you have gathered lies around as digital garbage in your head, always feeding your ego or idle mind?

Information can be used in your physical experiences. You as an electric body are constantly receiving information, you and only you can filter out what is relevant to your own personal growth and development.

[For your notes]

You, and only you, decide what information you will integrate into your physical life experience. All other information remains entertainment or useless distractions that disrupt not only your own physical health and well-being, but that of all those you have infected through your need to communicate or disseminate that information.

Information, on the other hand, can and does have an impact on and in our physical experience.

The more we focus on it, the more attention we pay to it, the more it alters consciousness and has a shifting impact in our physical and emotional reality.

[For your notes]

The more we focus on information, the more real it becomes, or just seems real (from mental and emotional to physical reality). Thoughts can become real manifestations within our physical experience as information is gathered through the five sense organs.

They affect your entire physical being. Starting with the surface tension of your skin, which is regulated by your emotional attachment to a particular piece of information.

As you floated in your mother's womb, or let's just say floated, you began to program your emotional attachment to the outside world and prepare for an existence as what defines "you" and your outside world as a human being.

[For your notes]

-breathe-

This definition is manipulated so that your subconscious and emotional body believe that the reality that your mother and or even her mother experienced and translated as absolute truth, as in their emotions, evolved into their own "One World" principles of reality that they believe in as a collective consciousness. This pre-programmed reality is very important to the physical existence of your first six years of life, after you have left the womb and expanded your memory.

„Memory grows indefinitely - Life for life“

Memory grows indefinitely life after life as you accept "death" as only a passing moment, the moment when you peacefully and graciously return what you have borrowed from Earth, namely your physical body.

You may wonder at this moment, as your illusory mind tries to imagine what it might mean to be faced now with something that is inevitable: "the absolute fact of the fragility of your existence."

Death is absolute, death is the end of breath.

Breathe inward and fill your lungs to full capacity, release the pressure, hold your breath

---one----two------three------four------five------ to 23

and then exhale very slowly, consciously releasing the waste or food for others in a fair trade and showing gratitude as you graciously complete your final trade.

This simple experience is one of the most powerful practices used by all great sages, saints, yogis, Buddhist monks and enlightened masters.

Each breathing cycle is an exercise or, as you might say, a preparation for the most exciting and inevitable moment that all of existence faces. In India and all Asian cultures there is a name for this process: "Soruba or Maha Samadhi".

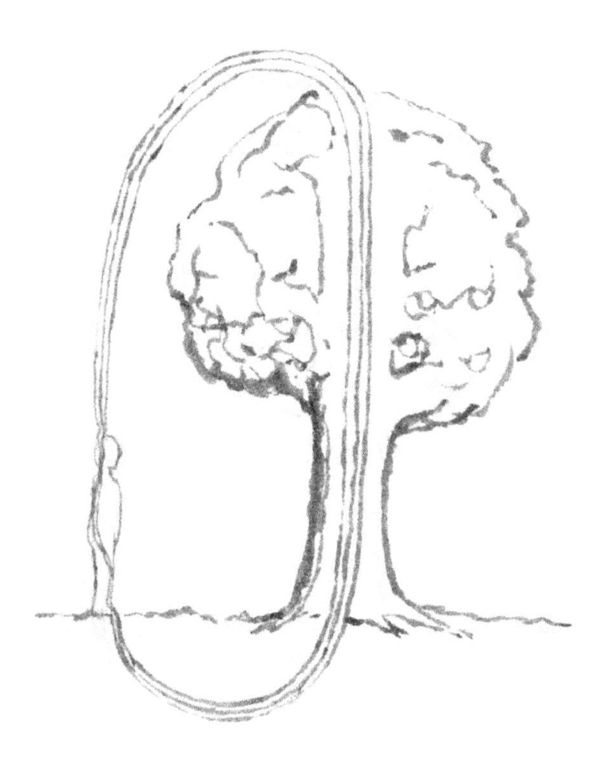

To achieve this "state of being," you practise the art of breathing, with each breath filled with bliss, a form of absolute gratitude.

You breathe inward, allowing every cell of your body to feel the exuberance and radiance of gratitude, then pause as your entire body absorbs this radiance.

Then, when you feel that you can no longer contain the radiant flow of energy, slowly breathe outward and fill your entire environment with this overwhelming gratitude without speaking or thinking.

Simply radiate joy, bliss, and gratitude while paying attention to the other half of your lungs, the trees, the plants, the animals, and all of our fellow human beings. With enough practice, you will develop a form of synchronicity with the entire universe as your consciousness expands.

[For your notes]

Breathe in, breathe out.

This process of "single existence" is the one that unites the well-being of all beings, even all material things, including plants, stars, the sun, even the entire universe with many universes.

The pulse of the "universal breath."

In samadhi, the yogi, the monk, the sage, leaves his physical form and does not cease to exist.

Again, "I" am using "your" imagination, fantasy and power to create what to you is as an illusion, but to me what "I" have described is the physical reality that is true in my physical life experiences.

[For your notes]

You may ask yourself the question, "Who are you," the one who pushes the ink-filled needle?" Or maybe you just stop reading and go outside the room you are currently occupying to experience the smiles on children's faces as you walk down the street to eat with your friends at your favourite pizza place.

[For your notes]

-breathe-

You may also choose to turn on your television, the Internet and other blinking crystals (blinking crystals are those that have been used to hypnotise you or fulfil the needs of "gathering information" that are currently in the physical reality of the entire human collective consciousness).

Never forget that you are also the vibrating energy field, the so-called "energy body" that emanates from your core.

[For your notes]

Breathe in

One---two----three----four----five-----six-----seven---24.

Pause, integrate, act, always aware of this physical connection.

The content of the information you gather affects your ability to communicate and how the information is interpreted. Your mind can design anything in virtual reality, it only needs the images your eyes have collected and the emotional memory.

Breathe out slowly; trade, feel lighter and lighter, you feel much younger; pause to show gratitude, life is just a matter of balance and emotion.

Excerpt/OriginalScript:

Happened. Something Every single [illegible]
Material Existence goes Through. a very very
small piece of "Male fire you call Light) Has
given you The signal To "Create".
you The Human Have
Begun your Existance in an Ocean, The
womb of your Mother. Within The first 3 Months
you Have Expeienced Every aspect of Evolution.

Egg / Sperm	3 days	1 week	[illegible] weeks	9 weeks	15 weeks	9 mon[illegible]

Collecting Particles To Create & Build A Hous[e]
For our souls. The Tree, The Roses, The worms, The
Fish, chickens, The grass That you Eat (Bread), Cow, Even
your own Car Began with The same Process as as
[illegible] Body of This Blue Ball spinning.

"I", the paper, carrier of the soul of the tree, the plant sap and the symbols have been happy to create this time with you.

Thank you for your attention and I look forward to accompanying you on your further journey

Thomas Arculeo / Séh-Shéh-yen-Goh / „White Eagle"

Born in Heidelberg (D) in 1957 to the highly respected Hupp couple of the North American Haudenosaunee (Iroquois), he grew up surrounded by his people for 17 years. Simultaneously with the intensive training in the school of life of his indigenous ancestry, he studied for seven years with his 74 year old teacher in Shaolin and Medical Qi-Gong. Over time, he worked with other teachers from India, Peru and Nigeria. Later, along with a job and family, came college studies in medicine and psychology, stints as a street worker in NY City and around the world.

The Iroquois have always been extremely politically engaged. Before an Iroquois can enter politics, he must have healed himself and mastered manifold teachings and studies. Thus, among the Iroquois, the office of chief, along with the roles of diplomat and advisor are occupied exclusively by spiritually and healingly educated people. Physically present in Europe for well over 200 years, Iroquois have acted as diplomats between cultures at royal houses and covertly with government officials.

About thirty years ago (October 1986) there was a Council of Elders of over 60 Indigenous Nations, including their Spiritual Leaders and Grandmothers in Hunter Mountain/New York State. There, the question was posed as to who would like to go to Europe. At first, no one came forward, as Europe was an extremely delicate terrain in this context. After discussions with the Grandmothers, Thomas finally decided to take on this responsible task. Since then, Thomas' ambitious goal has been to awaken indigenous consciousness in Europe and prepare the ground for this awakening.

We "Elders" convey a lived consciousness in connection with all forces of nature, which are always everywhere ready to serve us... but only if you are ready to accept this awakening responsibly....

Every creature has its position in the whole, only to serve the whole... Automatically this miracle happens, where suddenly the feeling of absolute security in the deepest inside takes over your being... to be one with nature in its wholeness... this only happens if you are willing to give up many conditionings and take the step that Mother Earth has provided for you... whether it is "vision quest" or Inner Journey, it is about your inner core of being awakened anew... like a small seed when it germinates.

We elders from the global indigenous community have decided to steadfastly occupy places in Europe where nature is fully intact... so that we can accompany and advise you....

Being here is valuable for your development as European Indigenous people... step by step it grows within you.... we Elders are only companions... we stand with you, beside you... not as leaders or guides... but as companions.... Being indigenous is one of the deepest inner processes of an individual who participates as part of a whole....

We are only companions of a very ancient knowledge guarded in the most difficult conditions....

Thomas Arculeo / Séh-Shéh-yen-Goh /" White Eagle"

Books- LIVING-CIRCLE.mittelstand.de:

www.mittelstand.de/shop

ISBN: 9783759750914

LIVING CIRCLE - Consciousness of the circle

MODEL CAMPUS FOR REVITALIZING

the European economic, cultural and social system.

The model campus for a prospering SME sector.
The education-oriented center for a creative resource community. Shaping the future - Exploiting today's opportunities with tomorrow's requirements and integrating them in a timely manner. Taking responsibility today for the life values of generations to come.

ISBN: 9783759759122

Peaceful solutions

The self-experiential introduction to the legacy of the Druids and Elders of the world. The entire series of books is a teaching path of the ancient way of the masters, as it was passed on orally in the past.
The author translates in writing what his masters have explained to him through oral traditions and examples of action.

Volume- 1 - Intro

Volume - 2 - I

Volume - 3 - We

Volume - 4 - The 5 elements

Volume - 5 - (0)

ISBN: 9783759759603

The Frog King & the children of Frya
- Volume 1

Fairy tales are messages from your ancestors.
The foundations of all peaceful civilizations on this earth.
The history of Europe and its circular culture.
The legacy of Europe's indigenous culture, explained in detail using language, codes and images.

The Frog King & the teachings of the children of Frya - Volume 2

The knowledge of indigenous European natural science and the background of their circle culture was the foundation of all peaceful advanced civilizations. It is time to bring this knowledge and these teachings back deeper into people's consciousness. The Frog Prince is the symbol for this process.
Fairy tales are messages from your ancestors.
The legacy of Europe's indigenous culture.

ISBN:9783759760012

A dandelion seed goes on a journey
Children's book

A hero's journey through the elements of life, showing courage, self-knowledge, inner power and the rich paths that life offers.
The story gives us strength and makes us realize how we can grow from apparent vulnerability to an unusual greatness. It is the impulse to take a closer look at the world again and to take a closer look.
It is the dragon within us that is awakened and the scientific wisdom of our ancestors, with which wonderful being we are connected.

A project by LIVING-CIRCLE.mittelstand.de

„Peaceful solutions“, Thomas Arculeo

Book orders:
www.mittelstand.de/buecher

More books:
www.mittelstand.de/shop
info@mittelstand.de

Contact:
info@mittelstand.de
thomas.arculeo@icloud.com

Academie:
www.mittelstand.de/akademie

Further projects:
LIVING-CIRCLE.mittelstand.de

European Indigenious Developement Centre:
EIDC.mittelstand.de